# picture me cooking

Recipes
have been created,
tested and approved with enthusiasm
by kids 3 to 103!!!

# Thanks

To Brad, Brit and Jake for being supportive and such good sports
during experimentation!   -AC

To Connor and Samantha – the inspiration for this journey.
John…thanks for the push!   -CK

To John, Meghan and Ryan, thanks for making time
in the kitchen so easy and fun!    -MP

To Tate, Carlyn and Avery, thanks for giving me all the
right ingredients to make cooking rock!   -RR

Art Direction by: Deb Early, www.debearlydesign.com
Photography by: Krista Bitting, www.kristabitting.com
Edited by: Andrea Kohalmi, Stephanie Zajkowski
Published by:  Picture Me Cooking, LLC.

Text Copyright © 2008, Picture Me Cooking, LLC.
Photography Copyright © 2008, Picture Me Cooking, LLC.
P.O. Box 41, Richboro PA 18954

Created in USA, Printed in China

ISBN 978-0-9821763-0-6

# How To Use This Book

*1.* Sit together and look over this book. See what looks interesting and decide which recipes to make first. We have provided a photo of each dish in the book to help your budding cooks get excited about what they want to make.

*2.* Have your camera ready to take photos of your chefs cooking. Take action shots, funny shots and shots of their creations.

*3.* Enjoy each success and laugh over mishaps. Later, slide chosen photos into the provided pockets. It's easy to update photos over the years - just slip another picture into the pocket.

**Picture Me Cooking** is more than just a cookbook or scrapbook; it is an heirloom in the making designed to capture a family's often overlooked moments in the kitchen. This book is also a great conversation piece to share with family and friends.

Our hope is that this book becomes one of your family keepsakes. Years from now when you and your family look through the worn and cherished pages and photographs, you will remember fond yet fleeting moments with warmth in your heart, a smile on your face, and maybe a laugh or two.

Consider having one book for each child to capture their individual experiences and triumphs in the kitchen - and to avoid deciding who gets to keep the family's recipe book in the future.

Children in the kitchen are excited to begin cooking
and they move quickly.
Cooking Buddies **cb** use your judgement
to ensure a fun and safe environment.

I received my first cookbook for Christmas when I was about nine years old. I can't recall the title, who helped me bake, or if there was a specific reason I created a "masterpiece" that day.

I do remember what my finished product looked like and how it made me feel. I created a Blizzard Cake—a popcorn covered chocolate cake with chocolate icing. (Yes, really!) As I anxiously presented it to my three brothers, sister, Mom and Dad, I couldn't wait to hear their reactions. I felt proud.  I felt confident. I felt important.

This was the moment that I fell in love with cooking. Even at that young age, I knew that cooking was an integral part of my family and that it was fun. (Thanks Mom!)

These days, I am often in the kitchen with my own little chefs who are also very proud of their creations. I fondly recall my Blizzard Cake and wish it had been "captured" so I could visually share it with my own family.

I began thinking about a way to capture my children's moments and "masterpieces" in the kitchen. I thought why not combine recipes with photos of their creations and moments in the kitchen. I mentioned the idea for this book to three of my friends. As moms themselves, they quickly became passionate about the project and the rest, as they say, is history!

Think of your children's pride as they complete this book. Years from now they will smile and laugh as they reminisce. They just might recreate some of their childhood favorites with their own children, making new memories.

Use this book with your children. Enjoy the special time it creates. Wear away the pages with frequent use. But most of all enjoy the memories it will hold for you and your families.

Colleen Kennedy

# Contents

# Hey Kids!

## Kitchen Rules for Safety and Success

Never cook alone. Always have a Cooking Buddy **cb** help you with the difficult parts of a recipe. Your Cooking Buddy **cb** should be an adult, like a parent, grandparent, aunt or uncle. *Cooking with someone else is always more fun!*

Helping hands need to be clean hands. Wet your hands with warm, running water, add some soap, rub your hands together to make lots of bubbles, and then rinse them well. Singing the ABC's or Happy Birthday while you wash helps you know when you have washed long enough to clean away any germs. *Germs are tricky!*

**Proper hand-washing technique with soap and water from the Mayo Clinic:**

1. Lather your hands with water and soap and rub them together vigorously for at least 15 to 20 seconds.
2. Scrub all surfaces, including the backs of your hands, wrists, between your fingers and under your fingernails.
3. Rinse well.
4. Dry your hands with a clean or disposable towel.
5. Use a towel to turn off the faucet.

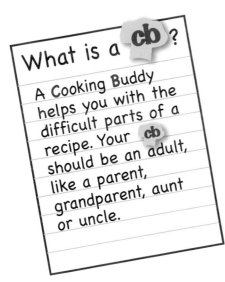

What is a **cb**?

A Cooking Buddy helps you with the difficult parts of a recipe. Your **cb** should be an adult, like a parent, grandparent, aunt or uncle.

If you have long hair, pull it back. You don't want your hair falling into the food. *Eeeeew!*

Always check expiration dates before you use foods. Every packaged food has an expiration or "use by" date on it. If the expiration date or freshness is questionable, do not use it. *When in doubt, throw it out!*

Be careful. Talk about the recipe with your **cb** first and discuss who will do each task. The more you cook, the more you will learn to do on your own. Be sure to use an oven mitt or potholder to touch or move hot pans or pots. Keep cords and appliances away from the sink or anywhere there is water. ***No need to get a shock.***

Clean up. It's easier to keep your workspace clean if you put things away after each step rather than waiting until the end. ***Use a trash bowl.***

Wash your hands after touching eggs, raw meat or anything sticky—remember to sing the ABC's or Happy Birthday.

Focus on what you are doing. If you are making two things, focus on one at a time for the best results.

Use a timer. Set it for a few minutes less than any recipe recommends. Ovens vary: you can always cook something a bit longer if needed. However, if something is overcooked, you can't fix it.

Take pictures of the things you cook and place them in this book so you can remember making each recipe.

Share the meals and treats you make with your family and friends. They will love it!

Be creative and have FUN!

# What is a Recipe?

A recipe is a written set of instructions that inspires and guides you in creating a chosen dish.

A recipe is broken down into two main parts:

*The ingredients* - what you need to have in order to make the dish.

*The instructions* - how to make the dish.

You should always read a recipe before you begin; this way you will know what to expect, how to prepare, how much help you will need and how much time to set aside.

After you have read your chosen recipe through, clear some space to work. This is called your workspace or prep area.

Next, gather your ingredients, tools and your cb. *Start Cooking!*

# Planning It Out

As a family, you can plan out your daily meals, special events and parties. Empower your children by enlisting their help in deciding what meals to prepare. Give each child the opportunity to be responsible for one meal in the coming week. They can be your shopping assistants by writing a grocery list and finding the ingredients at the store. Then spend quality time together by cooking as a family.

This powerful experience teaches:

| | |
|---|---|
| · Responsibility | · Nutrition |
| · Planning | · Adding |
| · Budgeting | · Measuring |
| · Writing | · Everyday science |
| · Reading | · Follow through and |
| · Shopping | project completion |

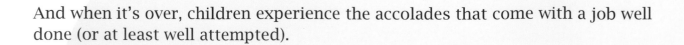

And when it's over, children experience the accolades that come with a job well done (or at least well attempted).

# Parents

## Did You Know?

By simply spending time in the kitchen, children learn decision-making, planning, organization and follow-up.

Recipes are useful for practicing reading and math while the chemistry of food provides a great first-hand lesson in science.

Cooking teaches children ownership and empowerment. Creating something and getting reviews on their finished product provides them with an immeasurable boost to their self-esteem. Your children will accomplish something they can see, taste and share.

Making meals and snacks with your children is an excellent way to teach them how to contribute to their family's needs.

Cooking with children teaches two essential life skills: communication and food preparation. Your children will utilize these skills for the rest of their lives (and thank you when they are on their own).

Children exercise creativity and get to learn by accident in a fun, creative, non-threatening environment.

Children will be more likely to try or taste something that they helped make.

Learning to cook and feeling comfortable in the kitchen can build confidence and help your children take on and overcome other challenges as they go through life.

Children are more likely to taste something they helped make!

# Kitchen Math

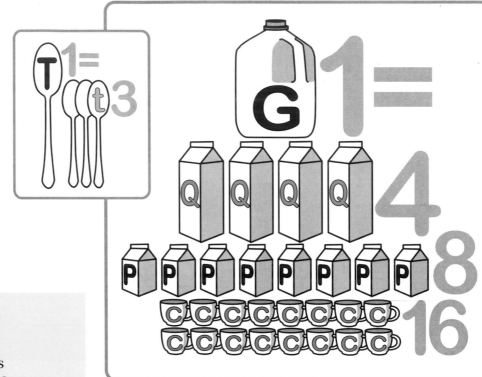

1 Quart = 2 Pints
1 Quart = 4 Cups
1 Pint = 2 Cups
1 Cup = 8 Ounces
½ Cup = 4 Ounces
1 Tablespoon = 3 Teaspoons
1 Pound = 16 Ounces

## Cooking Measurement Abbreviations

| Abbreviation | Measurement |
|---|---|
| tsp | teaspoon |
| Tbsp | tablespoon |
| fl | fluid |
| oz | ounce |
| pkg | package |
| pt | pint |
| qt | quart |
| gal | gallon |
| lb | pound |

## Converting Temperatures

### Fahrenheit to Celsius

1. Subtract 32 from degrees Fahrenheit
2. Multiply by 5
3. Divide by 9

### Celsius to Fahrenheit

1. Multiply degrees Celcius by 9
2. Divide by 5
3. Add 32

Only the United States and a few other countries (such as Belize) continue to use Fahrenheit as the accepted standard for non-scientific use. Most other countries have adopted Celsius as the primary scale in all use. Fahrenheit is sometimes used by older generations in English speaking countries, especially for measurement of higher temperatures and for cooking.

# Dinner Time = Family Time

**Gone are the days of daily family dinners.**

These days, at least one parent is usually working late or rushing home to whip something up for dinner. One or more of the kids have activities, the phone rings, the baby cries—we all know how it goes.

While it may be rare, it is a fantastic experience when the whole family can actually eat a nice dinner at a slow pace, talk about the day's events and plan for tomorrow.

Send a message to your kids – let the phone ring and plan a few nights each week to eat together. No matter what else is happening around each of you, show them that your family is a priority and they come first. It's a subtle lesson to learn and teach, but it will have a life-long impact as it lives on in their memories and they continue the tradition with their own families one day.

Preparing a family meal is much more memorable when kids either help or make it themselves. Cooking together and sharing breakfast, lunch or dinner together—these are the moments that often define and strengthen a family. Don't let them pass you by.

**Dig It Danish, 14**

**Mini Frittatas, 15**

**French Toast Kabobs, 17**

**Breakfast Parfait, 18**

French Toast Surprise, 16

# Sunrise Starters

Dig It Danish, 14

Mini Frittatas, 15

French Toast Surprise, 16

French Toast Kabobs, 17

Breakfast Parfait, 18

Egg Pie, 19

Egg Pie, 19

INSERT PHOTO

Easy to make and addictive to eat – a warm and scrumptious breakfast treat.

## INGREDIENTS

1 package crescent rolls

4 ounces cream cheese, softened (½ cup)

⅓ cup sugar

½ teaspoon vanilla

For Topping:

2 teaspoons sugar

¼ teaspoon cinnamon

Preheat oven to 350º.

1. Combine cream cheese, ⅓ cup of sugar and vanilla. Stir until smooth.

2. Separate crescent rolls into triangles. Spread a teaspoon of cream cheese mixture onto each triangle and then roll up wide end to pointed end.

3. Combine 2 tablespoons of sugar and ¼ teaspoon of cinnamon in a small bowl. Sprinkle the mixture over each danish.

4. Have **cb** put in the oven and bake for 10 – 12 minutes or until puffed-up and golden brown.

5. Once removed from oven, let cool for a few minutes. The filling will be very hot.

*Tip: Make it extra special by drizzling some strawberry jam over each danish. Mmmmmm!*

# Dig It Danish

# Mini Frittatas

What do you do when it's time for breakfast and everyone wants something different in his or her eggs? Make adorable individual frittatas of course! A frittata is an Italian dish similar to an omelet.

## INGREDIENTS

3 large eggs

¼ cup milk

A few dashes of salt and pepper

Butter

Combination ideas:

Cheese, cooked bacon

Vegetables: thin slices of zucchini or mushrooms, chopped onion, chopped pepper, broccoli. Anything your family might enjoy.

Preheat oven to 350°.

1. Using a muffin top pan or a cupcake pan, put a bit of butter on your fingers and grease each round you will be filling.

2. Whisk eggs, milk, salt and pepper.

3. Pour egg mixture into rounds filling ¾ of the way.

4. Sprinkle chosen toppings on the egg mixture in each round. Have **cb** place the pan in the oven.

5. Have **cb** cook 9 to 11 minutes if using a muffin top pan (preferred method). Cook for approximately 15 – 20 minutes if using a cupcake pan, until solid and golden brown.

6. Have **cb** remove from the oven and let stand for a couple of minutes to cool. Run a butter knife around the edges and use a fork to get under each frittata to gently lift it out.

*Tip: Keep a muffin top pan just for making frittatas; this will ensure a beautiful turnout every time.*

INSERT PHOTO

Breakfast

INSERT PHOTO

Not your typical French toast – kids love the twist. Plus, there is no need to use syrup!

## INGREDIENTS

1 egg

2 tablespoons of milk

½ cup strawberry jam

8-10 slices white bread

2 tablespoons powdered sugar

1 tablespoon butter

### Did You Know?

A fresh egg will sink in water but a stale egg will float.

1. Assemble "sandwiches" by spreading jam on a slice of bread and top it with another piece of bread.

2. Use a large cookie cutter to make fun shapes. Press the cutter firmly into each jam sandwich. For best results, cut out one sandwich at a time. Put your sandwich cut outs on a plate and set them aside until all the sandwiches are finished. Throw away (or eat) any leftover crusts.

3. Crack the egg (wash your hands after) into a small bowl and whisk it until blended. Add the milk and whisk it into the egg.

4. Have **cb** prepare a frying pan by putting a dab of butter in it and warming it over medium-high heat. Using a pastry brush or a spoon spread the egg mixture lightly on one side of each sandwich. Add the sandwiches egg-side down to the pan. Once you fill the pan, have **cb** quickly brush or spread the other side of the sandwiches with the egg mixture.

5. Have **cb** cook the sandwiches until they begin to brown and crisp (about 1 minute per side) and flip them over.

6. Remove from pan and place on plate. Add powdered sugar to a strainer and sprinkle it over all the sandwiches until they are lightly coated. Serve immediately.

# French Toast Surprise

# French Toast Kabobs

Sure you can have a shish kabob or a fruit kabob, but a breakfast kabob – now that's different!

## INGREDIENTS

5 large eggs, lightly beaten

½ cup milk

½ teaspoon vanilla

1 loaf unsliced white bread or Challah, crust mostly removed

½ pint fresh blueberries

½ pint fresh strawberries (raspberries or blackberries)

2 bananas

2 tablespoons butter (more or less as needed)

Maple syrup

Preheat oven to 200°.

1. Have **cb** place a baking sheet in the oven to warm.

2. Using a serrated knife, have **cb** help you remove the crust from the bread and then cut the bread into cubes.

3. Whisk eggs, milk and vanilla together in a medium bowl.

4. Have **cb** melt 1 tablespoon of butter in a skillet over low to medium heat.

5. Dip cubes into the egg mixture (in and out) and carefully place in the skillet.

6. Have **cb** cook half of the bread cubes, turning occasionally with a fork until browned on all sides.

7. Transfer the cooked bread cubes to the warmed baking sheet in the oven to keep warm.

8. Add remaining 1 tablespoon of butter to the skillet and repeat process until all the bread cubes are cooked.

9. Thread French toast cubes onto skewers alternating with fruit.

10. Drizzle kabobs with maple syrup and serve immediately.

*As you finish cooking each batch of French toast, place pieces in an oven safe dish and have **cb** put dish into your oven to keep warm.*

**Breakfast**

INSERT PHOTO

INSERT PHOTO

This is fun to make and good for you too. An easy way to surprise Mom or Dad with breakfast in bed!

## INGREDIENTS

8 ounces flavored yogurt for each parfait

1 or 2 fresh fruits of your choice, cleaned and sliced (blueberries, raspberries, strawberries or peaches) smaller berries remain whole

½ cup granola cereal like Kashi® GOLEAN Crunch Cereal

1. Place a large spoonful of granola in the glass and add ½ of the yogurt.

2. Cover the yogurt with more granola and top with fresh fruit.

3. Add the rest of the yogurt and top with granola and fruit.

*Tip: For best results use blended or whipped yogurt; do not use yogurt with fruit on the bottom. Strawberry, cherry, raspberry and blueberry work well.*

## Fun Facts

Blueberries are the 2nd most popular berry in the United States.

# Breakfast Parfait

# Egg Pie

This is so good, it's sure to be a crowd pleaser! Perfect for a lazy Sunday or a holiday morning breakfast. Plus it reheats well.

## INGREDIENTS

1 frozen or fresh deep dish uncooked pie crust

3 eggs

1 ½ cups whole milk

½ cup chopped broccoli (frozen works well; just thaw, drain, and blot dry)

1 cup chopped ham

6 ounces shredded Cheddar cheese

1 tablespoon flour

1 tablespoon butter, melted

Dash or two of salt and pepper

Preheat oven to 375°.

1. Have **cb** help you place the piecrust into a deep pie pan or dish (or purchase a deep dish pie crust in a tin). Press on the dough to form it to the bottom and sides of your pan.

2. Place the pie pan on a baking sheet which will catch any drips and keep your **cb** from scrubbing the bottom of the oven later.

3. Whisk together the milk, eggs, salt, pepper, butter and flour. Add in the ham, broccoli and cheese.

4. Pour mixture into the piecrust. Be careful not to overfill.

5. Have **cb** place pie in the oven for 45 to 50 minutes. Pie should be puffed-up and golden brown on top. When done, have **cb** remove pie from the oven.

6. Allow the pie to stand for 10 minutes before cutting and serving.

*You can use any combination of your favorite veggies and cheese. Leftovers are easily transported and can be reheated in a microwave – great for lunch at school or work.*

INSERT PHOTO

Breakfast

**Strawberry Whirl, 22**

**Fizzy, 23**

**Candy Cane Cocoa, 25**

**Choc-O-Pops, 26**

# Delicious Drinks

Mix It Milkshake, 24

Summer Spritzer, 27

21

INSERT PHOTO

Who knew getting your vitamins and minerals could taste so good?

## INGREDIENTS

2 cups milk

8 ounces frozen strawberries in syrup

¼ cup sugar

¼ teaspoon vanilla

**Whipped Cream** (optional)

1. Have **cb** help you place all ingredients into a blender. Blend until smooth.

2. Pour into glasses. Add a straw and serve.

**Homemade Whipped Cream**
Small container of heavy or light whipping cream
1 ½ tablespoons sugar

1. Add a small container of heavy or light whipping cream (found in the milk section at your supermarket) to a medium-sized bowl.

2. Using a hand mixer or stationary mixer whip the cream on medium high until stiff peaks begin to form.

3. Add 1½ tablespoons sugar—more or less to taste. Whip for another 30 seconds.

*Believe me…making your own whipped cream is worth the extra few minutes. Plus, it makes a great science lesson; the addition of air bubbles changes the cream from a liquid to an almost solid.*

# Strawberry Whirl

# Fizzy

Add a little fizz and sophistication to your favorite juice. Great for lunch with friends, a tea party or as a special birthday punch.

## INGREDIENTS

1 small can lemon-lime soda

2 cups juice – strawberry based such as a strawberry-kiwi

4 glasses

### Showstopper
Blueberries
Raspberries
Strawberries

1. Pour ¼ can of the soda into each glass.

2. Add ½ cup of the juice.

3. Adjust to your liking.

*For a "showstopper" effect, make your own ice cubes in advance. Fill an ice cube tray ½ way with the juice you will be using, then add some blueberries, raspberries or sliced strawberries. This way your drink will stay cold, not get diluted and when you're finished you have a fruit surprise to eat.*

## Fun Facts
California and Arizona produce 95% of the United States lemon crop.

Drinks

INSERT PHOTO

INSERT PHOTO

In the mood for a milkshake?  Make your own!  Try any combination from your imagination. Drink with a straw or eat with a spoon, you decide.

## INGREDIENTS

1 pint ice cream

¼ cup milk

½ teaspoon vanilla extract

Add in ideas:

Chocolate chips or your favorite cookie, crumbled

Sprinkles, cake and icing

Chocolate or strawberry syrup

Brownie, crumbled

Banana, cut

1. Have **cb** help you place ice cream and milk in your blender.  Blend until smooth.

2. Add in something from the list or from your imagination. Mix well. Pour into glasses and enjoy.

*Of course, you can use any flavor of ice cream – just omit the vanilla and enjoy your creation.*

### Did You Know?

Why aren't bananas ever lonely?

They hang out in bunches!

# Mix It Milkshake

# Candy Cane Cocoa

After some fun in the snow, this festive cocoa warms you up fast. This is the perfect way to turn an ordinary, cold winter day into a memorable one.

## INGREDIENTS

4 cups milk

2 ounces chocolate chips

3 crushed candy canes

4 small candy canes
for garnish (optional)

**Whipped cream**
(see page 22)

1. Crush 3 candy canes - add them to a sealable plastic bag and pound with a spoon or a rolling pin or simply have **cb** help you toss the candy canes into blender and press the crush button.

2. Have **cb** help you heat the milk in a saucepan over low to medium heat until hot, do not boil. Remove from heat.

3. Carefully whisk in chocolate chips and crushed candy canes until all are melted and smooth.

4. Have **cb** pour into mugs. Top with **Whipped Cream** (page 22) and a bit of additional crushed candy cane and serve.

*For added fun and flavor, use a mini candy cane as a stirrer.*

## Fun Facts

The candy cane was first introduced to America in 1847 by a German-Swedish immigrant by the name of August Imgard.

INSERT PHOTO

**Drinks**

INSERT PHOTO

A drink you can eat!

INGREDIENTS

Chocolate milk*
Popsicle molds

1. Pour chocolate milk into popsicle molds.

2. Freeze for at least 3 hours. Pop out and enjoy!

*If making your own chocolate milk use a good amount of chocolate syrup and for best results use 1% milk.

*Tip: For perfect pops, run the mold under warm water first before you pull them out.*

## Fun Facts

Why is milk white? Milk contains casein. It's the milk protein that is rich in calcium and it's white. The cream in milk has some fat which is also white. These two make milk white.

# Choc-O-Pops

# Summer Spritzer

It's easy to turn this into something fun or elegant with special glasses and straws. On a hot summer day, cool off with this sunshine in a glass.

## INGREDIENTS

6 cups cold water

6 – 8 lemons, washed

¾ cup sugar

½ cup lemon-lime soda or ginger ale

3 – 4 strawberries, washed and sliced

¼ cup blueberries, washed

12 grapes, washed and halved

3 thin slices of lemons, washed

1. Pour cold water into a large pitcher.

2. Juice the lemons and add to the pitcher filled with water.

3. Mix in the sugar until it's dissolved and chill the lemonade in the refrigerator until cold.

4. When ready to serve, add lemon-lime soda or ginger ale to the pitcher.

5. Add a combination of the fresh fruit to the bottom of each glass.

6. Fill the glasses with lemonade.

*Make this extra fun by adding a ¼ to ½ teaspoon of blue or green gelatin powder to your pitcher for a quick color change. Stir well.*

*Tip: To prevent lemon seeds in your drink, place a strainer over your pitcher or bowl when squeezing the lemons.*

INSERT PHOTO

Drinks

**Awesome Apple Dip, 30**

**CK's Cone Mix, 31**

**Luck O' The Irish Bread, 33**

**Scavenger Hunt Mix, 34**

**Brownie Cookies, 35**

**Fruit Salsa, 36**

Party Pineapple, 32

# Snackage

Banana Bread Bites, 37

29

INSERT PHOTO

This is ridiculously good! Let's see if an apple a day truly keeps the doctor away!

## INGREDIENTS

2 large apples such as Granny Smith or Macintosh (or use one of each)

1 teaspoon sugar

Cinnamon

**Mexican Dessert Chips**
(See p.36)

1. Wash apples, then have **cb** help you peel, core and chop them into small pieces. (You can use butter knives to chop apples – even plastic knives will do the trick.)

2. In a small bowl, mix sugar and a dash or two of cinnamon (to taste), sprinkle over apples and stir until evenly coated.

3. Serve with **Mexican Dessert Chips**. (see page 36)

*Tip: If you are not eating this right away, sprinkle apples with a bit of lemon juice and cover. Place chips in a sealed plastic bag.*

### Did You Know?

Apples are a member of the rose family.

# Awesome Apple Dip

# CK's Cone Mix

One of the boys favorites, it's a perfect snack for kids. It travels well for picnics, hikes or playground visits. Plus you get to eat the bowl!

## INGREDIENTS

Ice cream cones
Raisins
Dried cranberries
Chocolate chips
Your favorite cereal(s)
Mini pretzel sticks
Mini marshmallows

1. Mix a handful of your chosen ingredients in a bowl or plastic bag.

2. Fill cone(s).

*You can add anything that you like in place of the suggested ingredients. Try sunflower seeds, peanuts, banana chips, mini candies or any dried fruit. Your options are endless so you can please even the pickiest eater.*

*Tip: For easier transportation when you're on the go, leave this mixture in a bag and fill cones when ready.*

### Did You Know?

A waffle booth owned by Ernest Hamwi at the 1904 St Louis Worlds Fair was next to an ice cream vendor who ran short of dishes in which to put his ice cream. Ernest stepped in and rolled a waffle to contain the ice cream instead and the ice cream cone was born! Thank goodness!

INSERT PHOTO

**Snackage**

INSERT PHOTO

Surprise your family and friends with this fabulously unique appetizer. It's a centerpiece you can eat!

## INGREDIENTS

1 whole pineapple

Cheese cut into 1-inch cubes

Bite sized balls of mozzarella

Grape tomatoes

Salami cut into 1-inch cubes

Pepperoni cut into 1-inch cubes

Olives

Grapes

Cantaloupe and/or honeydew melon cut into 1-inch cubes

Toothpicks

*Use any or all of the above to decorate your pineapple.*

1. Rinse pineapple, tomatoes and grapes. Pat dry.

2. Thread just one or several food items onto a toothpick. Set aside on a plate.

3. Using a metal skewer, poke holes into the pineapple in places where you will insert the toothpicks.

4. Insert completed toothpicks in pre-made holes around pineapple.

5. Serve immediately or refrigerate for up to 2 hours.

*Instead of a pineapple, you can also use a whole cantaloupe, honeydew or watermelon. If the melon isn't steady on a flat surface, have* **cb** *slice just a bit off the bottom.*

*Tip: These days a lot of schools do not allow cupcakes for birthdays – make one of these with all fruit; it's sure to be a hit.*

# Party Pineapple

# Luck O' The Irish Bread

This is a nice way to welcome a new neighbor or to give as a gift to someone special. This recipe reminds us of some great family memories. We make it in our great grandmother's cast iron skillet that is almost 100 years old.

## INGREDIENTS

4 ½ cups
all purpose flour

1 ¼ cup sugar

2 ½ teaspoons
baking powder

½ teaspoon salt

1 teaspoon baking soda

½ cup (1 stick) butter,
softened or melted

2 ½ cups raisins

2 ½ cups buttermilk

1 large egg

Preheat oven to 350°.

1. Use a 10 – 12 inch ovenproof skillet with 2 – 2 ½ inch sides or 2 cake pans. Cut a circle of parchment paper to line the bottom of the pan(s).

2. Whisk first five ingredients in a large bowl to blend.

3. Add butter and raisins. Stir well.

4. In a measuring cup or small bowl, whisk buttermilk and egg. Add to flour mixture and stir with a large wooden spoon until all ingredients are just incorporated and it forms a dough ball. Do not over mix.

5. Place in pan(s) and shape into a dome.

6. Have **cb** bake for one hour or until top is brown and a wooden skewer or butter knife comes out clean after inserted into the middle.

*There is almost nothing better than a slice of Irish Soda Bread hot out of the oven with a smear of butter! Later, warm a slice in the microwave and enjoy. This is a big loaf; so make it in two pans and share with a friend or neighbor hot from the oven.*

*Tip: If making 2 smaller loaves, set timer for 45 minutes then do the toothpick test.*

Snackage

INSERT PHOTO

INSERT PHOTO

**cb** – Place ingredients in sealed bags and hide around the house or outside. Have kid(s) hunt for the ingredients, then mix it up and enjoy eating it as the reward.

## INGREDIENTS

3 cups wheat cereal squares

3 cups corn or rice cereal squares

3 cups crunchy cinnamon and honey cereal squares

½ pound mini pretzels or snaps

1 cup mixed nuts or your favorite nut (optional)

½ teaspoon cinnamon

2 tablespoons vegetable oil

2 pounds white chocolate melting disks (found at craft stores and some supermarkets)

1. In a very large bowl or pot, mix together cereals, pretzels and nuts.

2. With your **cb** 's help, melt the white chocolate disks in a double boiler or in the microwave stirring frequently until smooth. Remove from heat and stir in cinnamon and oil.

3. Have **cb** pour white chocolate sauce over mix and stir until evenly coated.

4. Pour mix onto parchment or wax paper lined baking sheet and let dry. (To speed up drying, place in the refrigerator for 30 minutes.)

5. Break into pieces and store in a sealed container.

*This freezes well, but there are rarely any leftovers!*

*The beauty of a mix is that you can mix in whatever you like...chocolate-coated candies, raisins, dried fruits, your favorite cereals – whatever.*

# Scavenger Hunt Mix

# Brownie Cookies

One New Year's Eve we were curious about turning brownies into cookies. It worked and now each cookie is like the best part of the brownie...the crispy edges!

## INGREDIENTS

1 package brownie mix (and ingredients as stated on package, usually oil and eggs)

2 tablespoons flour

¼ teaspoon baking powder

### Fun Facts

The Cacao Tree, which is native to South America, produces pods which hold the seeds (often called beans) that are the source of cocoa and chocolate.

Preheat oven to 350°.

1. Follow instructions on brownie package then mix in the flour and baking powder.

2. Stir until all ingredients are fully mixed.

3. On a parchment paper* lined baking sheet, place a tablespoon of batter for each cookie. Allow two inches of space between cookies.

4. Have cb place baking sheet in the oven and bake for 8 - 10 minutes or until the middle of the cookies are set.

5. Let the cookies cool on the baking sheet for 1 - 2 minutes then remove with spatula and cool completely on cooling racks.

*Variations:* You can add sprinkles or chocolate chips to these as well prior to baking - create your own unique cookie.

* Do not substitute wax paper for parchment paper.

Snackage

INSERT PHOTO

INSERT PHOTO

Take a trip to a farm stand or market and see which fruit looks good. Make a sweet snack, starter or dessert. Who knew fruit could taste so good?

## INGREDIENTS

2 Granny Smith apples, peeled and chopped into cubes

1 pint strawberries, chopped into cubes

1 pint blueberries

2 tablespoons sugar

3 tablespoons strawberry jam

1 teaspoon lemon juice

Graham crackers or **Mexican Dessert Chips** (recipe on right)

1. Combine all of the fruit together in a medium size bowl.

2. Stir the sugar, strawberry jam and lemon juice in a separate bowl until combined. Pour over the fruit, mix, cover and chill for ½ hour.

3. Serve with graham crackers or **Mexican Dessert Chips**.

**Mexican Dessert Chips**
3 eight-inch flour tortillas
2 tablespoons melted butter
2 tablespoons sugar
¼ teaspoon cinnamon

Preheat oven to 350º.

1. In a small bowl, mix sugar with several dashes of cinnamon (to taste). Set aside.

2. Lightly brush melted butter over tortillas.

3. Have **cb** cut tortillas into 6 slices (try using a pizza cutter).

4. Sprinkle each slice with cinnamon-sugar mixture.

5. Have **cb** bake on a baking sheet for 5 – 8 minutes or until crisp.

# Fruit Salsa

# Banana Bread Bites

Soon you will wait with anticipation for your bananas to brown.
Buy extra bananas so you can always have some ready to go!

## INGREDIENTS

3 - 4 (browning) bananas, peeled and mashed

2 cups all purpose flour

1 teaspoon baking soda

½ teaspoon salt

½ cup butter, softened

1 cup sugar

2 eggs

⅓ cup milk

1 teaspoon lemon juice

¾ cup chocolate chips

Preheat oven to 350º.

1. Mix flour, salt and baking soda in a medium bowl. Set aside.

2. In a small mug or bowl, combine milk and lemon juice. Set aside.

3. In a large bowl, cream butter and sugar. Add eggs, bananas and milk mixture. Stir well.

4. Add the flour mixture and the chocolate chips. Stir well.

5. Lightly coat a mini-muffin pan with cooking spray or line with baking cups.

6. Fill each cup ¾ full. Have **cb** cook for about 10 - 15 minutes. To check on muffins, have **cb** insert a wooden toothpick into one muffin. If it comes out clean, they're done.

*Variation: For a moist and delicious loaf of Banana Bread, use a loaf pan and cook at 350° for 50 - 60 minutes or until a toothpick comes out clean. When cooled a bit, just slice and serve. Your house will smell wonderful!*

**Snackage**

INSERT PHOTO

**Pepperoni Bread, 40**

**Sweet N' Crunchy Chicken, 41**

**Magic Sandwiches, 42**

**Grandpa's Pasta Pockets, 43**

**Tomato Pots, 45**

**Mucho Nachos, 46**

# Midday Morsels

Lunchtime Crostini, 44

Seashell Sandwiches, 47

INSERT PHOTO

Lunchtime, dinner time, snack time, anytime – this is sure to please!

## INGREDIENTS

1 loaf frozen bread dough, defrosted

1 egg, beaten

½ cup sliced pepperoni (more or less to taste)

1 cup shredded mozzarella cheese

4 tablespoons grated Parmesan cheese

1 tablespoon oregano (optional)

Pizza or tomato sauce (optional)

Lightly grease baking sheet. Preheat oven to 350°.

1. Roll dough into shape of a rectangle. Brush with beaten egg.

2. Cover the dough with pepperoni. Sprinkle mozzarella cheese, Parmesan cheese and oregano on top of the dough and pepperoni.

3. Have **cb** help you roll up the dough firmly like a jelly roll or wrap.

4. Pinch the seam to seal it. Place the dough seal side down on a lightly greased baking sheet.

5. Ask **cb** to bake for 35 to 40 minutes. Bread will be golden.

6. Have **cb** remove the bread from the oven. Let it cool for 5 minutes then slice it and serve it with pizza sauce for dipping.

*Variation: Pizza Bread—Spread sauce on the dough before adding the pepperoni and cheeses.*

# Pepperoni Bread

# Sweet N' Crunchy Chicken

Have you ever combined breakfast and dinner? Now you can! You will enjoy crushing cereal a bit with your fingers, then coating the chicken.

## INGREDIENTS

1 pound thin strips of boneless chicken

2 tablespoons mayonnaise, placed in a small bowl

1 cup sweetened cornflake cereal, crushed a bit

Preheat oven to 350°.

1. Lightly oil a baking sheet or dish. Put a dab of oil on a paper towel and rub over pan.

2. Have **cb** cut chicken into strips.

3. Using your hands, grab some mayo out of the bowl and coat chicken with it - just a little bit. Immediately roll in sweetened cornflakes and place on baking sheet.

4. Have **cb** bake for 15-20 minutes, depending on the thickness of your strips.

*Singing the ABC's when you wash your hands is a good practice to ensure good cleaning! Don't forget to wash the tops of your hands and wrists too!*

**Proper hand-washing technique with soap and water from the Mayo Clinic:**

1. Lather your hands with water and soap and rub them together vigorously for at least 15 to 20 seconds.
2. Scrub all surfaces, including the backs of your hands, wrists, between your fingers and under your fingernails.
3. Rinse well.
4. Dry your hands with a clean or disposable towel.
5. Use a towel to turn off the faucet.

INSERT PHOTO

**Midday Morsels**

INSERT PHOTO

What's the magic? They disappear!

## INGREDIENTS

10 slices of sliced white or wheat bread

Your favorite jelly or jam

Peanut butter (optional)

### Fun Facts

It takes about 550 peanuts to make a 12-ounce jar of creamy peanut butter.

1. Spread 5 slices of bread with your jelly/jam/peanut butter.

2. Top with remaining bread to make sandwiches.

3. Use your favorite cookie cutter shapes to cut out your "magic sandwiches." Press the cookie cutter firmly into the sandwich and wiggle it around to remove the ends. Place the sandwiches onto plates and serve.

*Great for picnics! Use any filler you choose...cheese, ham and cheese, fluff and peanut butter, cream cheese and cucumbers, what ever you like.*

*Tip: If your bread is thick, you might want to first cut out shapes and then spread jelly/peanut butter on one half and top with another...little ones can play the match game.*

# Magic Sandwiches

# Grandpa's Pasta Pockets

Get ready for two kid favorites...rolls and spaghetti!

## INGREDIENTS

2 fresh French bread
loaves (or Italian)
½ pound spaghetti
Sauce

**Fun Facts**

America's first
pasta factory
was built in
Brooklyn, NY.
The fresh pasta
was spread on
the roof to dry.

1. Have **cb** help you cut the loaves in half. Using a knife, have **cb** cut out the inside of the rolls to make the pockets. (Note to **cb** : Twist a knife in a circular motion or use a fork to scrape out the insides.) Do your best to keep from putting holes in the roll.

2. Have **cb** help you cook the spaghetti according to the directions on the package and then drain the pasta. Toss with sauce and gently begin to fill bread pockets. Push the pasta mixture down into the bread pocket to allow more spaghetti to fit inside.

3. Pick them up and take a bite.

*Once hollowed out, you can stuff your "pocket" with any pasta. Try it with butter sauce, olive oil or tomato sauce. Go all out and add sausages and peppers, chicken or* **Mini Meatballs** *(p.51). You can even throw in a Caesar or mixed green salad tossed with dressing.*

INSERT PHOTO

**Midday Morsels**

INSERT PHOTO

Endless possibilities and perfect for a crowd.

### INGREDIENTS

1 loaf of French or Italian bread

Any of the following: Jelly, jam, peanut butter, ham, cheese, turkey, cream cheese spread, tuna fish, chicken salad, or applesauce with apple slices are some ideas

1. Have **cb** help you slice bread into ¼ inch thick slices.

2. Place topping(s) of your choice on each slice and serve them like open-face sandwiches.

*Serve on a tiered platter for teatime fun or place a few varieties on a large platter and scatter grapes and berries around the sandwiches to make a more festive and scrumptious presentation.*

### Did You Know?

In France, French bread is called "une baguette" which means stick or wand.

# Lunchtime Crostini

# Tomato Pots

These are pretty, tasty and fun to make – great for lunch or a side dish.

## INGREDIENTS

6 medium tomatoes

3 cups of shredded Cheddar cheese – or a Tex-Mex combination

1 teaspoon taco seasoning

4 ounces canned, diced mild green chilies (they give flavor and are not spicy. Look for them in your supermarket's Mexican food section)

Grease baking sheet. Preheat oven to 350º.

1. Wash and dry the tomatoes. Have **cb** help you slice the top off each tomato. Using the small end of a melon baller or spoon, scrape out most of each tomato's insides. Be careful not to break through the sides or bottom.

2. Turn the tomato pots upside down and place onto paper towels, allowing them to drain for 30 minutes.

3. In a medium bowl, toss cheese, chilies and taco seasoning. Stuff each tomato.

4. Place the stuffed tomatoes on the lightly greased baking sheet. Have **cb** put it in the oven.

5. Bake tomatoes for 15 to 20 minutes or until cheese begins to bubble.

6. Have **cb** remove the tray from the oven.

*Variations: Fill each tomato with macaroni and cheese or homemade/store-bought chili, which you can top with cheese and sour cream.*

INSERT PHOTO

INSERT PHOTO

Have fun building your nachos, then just pick up and eat.

## INGREDIENTS

30 large tortilla chips

1½ cups shredded Cheddar cheese or Tex-Mex cheese

Preheat oven to 350°.

1. Place tortillas in a single layer on a foil lined baking sheet. (The foil makes clean up much easier.)

2. Sprinkle each tortilla with cheese.

3. Have **cb** place the tray in the oven and bake for 5 minutes or until the cheese is melted.

*Serve immediately. These are yummy by themselves or serve them with some salsa and sour cream for dipping.*

### Did You Know?

It is believed that salsa dates back to the 15th century Aztec Indians.

# Mucho Nachos

# Seashell Sandwiches

A cool twist on a <u>sand</u>wich.

## INGREDIENTS

12 large pasta shells

Tuna salad or
chicken salad

Grapes, washed

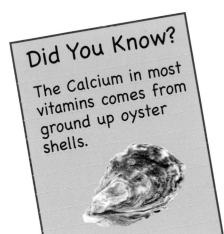

**Did You Know?**

The Calcium in most vitamins comes from ground up oyster shells.

1. Have **cb** cook shells following the directions on the package. Drain, toss with a few drops of olive oil and cool, then line up on a baking sheet.

2. Stuff each shell with the salad of your choice, place on serving plates and decorate with a branch of grapes.

*Variation: Prepare your favorite garden salad or Caesar salad; chop it up, toss it with dressing, then stuff it in the shells. Arrange on a plate lined with lettuce and scatter grape tomatoes around for color—and eating of course! Enjoy these as finger food or for less mess use a fork.*

INSERT PHOTO

**Cluckers, 50**

**Mini Meatballs, 51**

**Tortellini Skewers, 53**

**Garlic and Rosemary Chicken, 54**

**Make Your Own Pizza, 56**

**Spaghetti Salad, 57**

Shark Bites, 52

# Let's Do Dinner

Nana Noodles, 55

Peek-A-Boo Salad, 58

What's YOUR Noodle Soup?, 59

INSERT PHOTO

These little bundles go down quick and easy, so make extra!

## INGREDIENTS

Purchased or homemade pie or pizza dough, enough for 2 crusts

2 tablespoons chopped onion

3 tablespoons butter

3 tablespoons chicken broth

1 ½ cups cooked chicken, shredded

¼ teaspoon garlic salt

Few dashes of pepper (optional)

4 ounces of cream cheese

*This one takes a little work, so preheat oven to 375° while you are rolling out the dough.*

1. Have **cb** sauté onion in butter in a large skillet until tender. Stir in chicken, chicken broth, garlic salt, pepper and cream cheese. Remove from heat and set aside for step 3.

2. Place a piece of wax or parchment paper under the piecrust and over the piecrust. Roll out until 1/16 inch thick. Using a 3-inch biscuit or cookie cutter, cut out as many circles as you can. Gather remaining scraps, form back into a ball, press down between wax or parchment paper and repeat.

3. Fill the center of each round with a heaping teaspoon of filling. Fold over gently and press down slightly on filling. Pinch edges or use a fork to seal. If you happen to have an empanada crimp, that works well too. Gently prick each Clucker with a toothpick two times for small steam vents.

4. Have **cb** place Cluckers on an ungreased baking sheet and bake for 15-20 minutes or until they are a golden brown.

*These freeze well, so make a double batch.*

# Cluckers

# Mini Meatballs

Make these minis to serve over pasta, on a roll or by themselves.

## INGREDIENTS

1 pound of ground beef

½ cup seasoned breadcrumbs

1 egg

2 tablespoons Parmesan cheese

1 tablespoon milk

Fresh or dried garlic to taste (optional)

A few dashes of salt and pepper

Tomato sauce

Preheat oven to 350º.

1. In a large bowl, combine all ingredients except tomato sauce.

2. Use your clean hands to mix until everything is fully combined.

3. Use a teaspoon and scoop out bits of the mixture. Use your hands to form into small 1-inch balls by rolling mixture around in your palms.

4. Have **cb** help you place meatballs on a lightly oiled baking sheet and bake for 8-12 minutes or until browned.

5. Once removed from the oven, place in a pot of tomato sauce. Have **cb** cook over low heat for 10 minutes and serve.

**Proper hand-washing technique with soap and water from the Mayo Clinic:**

1. Lather your hands with water and soap and rub them together vigorously for at least 15 to 20 seconds.
2. Scrub all surfaces, including the backs of your hands, wrists, between your fingers and under your fingernails.
3. Rinse well.
4. Dry your hands with a clean or disposable towel.
5. Use a towel to turn off the faucet.

INSERT PHOTO

**Dinner**

INSERT PHOTO

A cool mini burger that comes from the sea!

## INGREDIENTS

Package of small dinner rolls or mini Kaiser rolls

1 lb fresh tuna, cut into chunks

¼ cup soy sauce

1 teaspoon Worcestershire sauce

1 tablespoon whole grain or Dijon mustard

½ cup breadcrumbs

1 green onion, chopped fine (optional)

1 tablespoon fresh ginger root, chopped fine

1. Have **cb** help you use a mini or full sized food processor to grind tuna. A few pulses should do it. Add in the breadcrumbs and pulse until combined.

2. Scrape into a medium bowl and add in the rest of the ingredients. Stir with a spatula until mixed.

3. Form into mini burgers. Place on a plate, cover and refrigerate until ready to grill.

4. Have **cb** grill on medium heat for 3-4 minutes a side.

*Serve on mini rolls with horseradish sauce or a bit of mustard.*

**Proper hand-washing technique with soap and water from the Mayo Clinic:**

1. Lather your hands with water and soap and rub them together vigorously for at least 15 to 20 seconds.
2. Scrub all surfaces, including the backs of your hands, wrists, between your fingers and under your fingernails.
3. Rinse well.
4. Dry your hands with a clean or disposable towel.
5. Use a towel to turn off the faucet.

# Shark Bites

# Tortellini Skewers

Somehow eating food off a stick makes it taste even better!

## INGREDIENTS

½ pound fresh cheese tortellini (from refrigerated section)

½ teaspoon olive oil

Spaghetti sauce for dipping

Small wooden skewers or toothpicks

1. Have **cb** help you cook tortellini according to package directions.

2. Have **cb** drain and place tortellini in a medium bowl. Toss with olive oil, cover and let sit for a few minutes until cool enough for safe handling.

3. Thread a few tortellini on wooden toothpicks or small skewers and arrange on a plate.

4. Put a small bowl of heated sauce in the middle of a large platter, place skewers all around and serve.

*Tip: Make some **Mini Meatballs** (pg. 51) and serve on skewers/toothpicks as well. Mix it up…make some skewers with a meatball, some with tortellini and some with both.*

## Fun Facts

There are more than 600 pasta shapes produced worldwide!

Dinner

INSERT PHOTO

INSERT PHOTO

An easy chicken dish that will make your kitchen smell delicious!!

## INGREDIENTS

5-6 cloves of garlic
(more if desired)

3 sprigs fresh rosemary

3-4 boneless
chicken breasts

⅓ cup olive oil

### Fun Facts

Garlic was fed to Roman Soldiers to make them "strong and courageous".

Preheat oven to 350º.

1. Have **cb** help you peel the garlic cloves and set aside.

2. In a baking dish, combine oil, garlic, whole rosemary sprigs and chicken. Cover with foil.

3. Have **cb** place in oven and cook for 30 minutes.

*Tip: You can serve this alongside or over buttered noodles. Add in a nice loaf of French bread or some Salad Cups (pg. 63) and you have a meal.*

**Proper hand-washing technique with soap and water from the Mayo Clinic:**

1. Lather your hands with water and soap and rub them together vigorously for at least 15 to 20 seconds.
2. Scrub all surfaces, including the backs of your hands, wrists, between your fingers and under your fingernails.
3. Rinse well.
4. Dry your hands with a clean or disposable towel.
5. Use a towel to turn off the faucet.

# Garlic and Rosemary Chicken

# Nana Noodles

When Nana Coopersmith puts this family favorite on the table, the kids come running!

## INGREDIENTS

½ pound thin spaghetti or thin egg noodles, uncooked

4 tablespoons butter

2 cups instant rice, uncooked

2 cans French onion soup (undiluted), strain out the onion pieces

2 cans chicken broth

1 cup water

1 tablespoon soy sauce

Preheat oven to 350º.

1. Have **cb** help you sauté the dry noodles in butter over medium-low heat until brown, approximately 5-7 minutes.

2. Have **cb** drain off excess butter.

3. Place all ingredients in a casserole dish.

4. Cover dish with foil, have **cb** place in the oven and cook for 30 minutes. Stir and cook an additional 15-20 minutes.

*Tip: This can be frozen and reheats well.*

INSERT PHOTO

Dinner

INSERT PHOTO

What's your favorite part...the making or the eating?

## INGREDIENTS

8-inch flour tortillas

Olive oil

Pizza sauce

Shredded mozzarella cheese

Preheat oven to 400°.

1. Place tortillas on baking sheets. Put a small amount of olive oil on your clean hands and lightly rub over top of each tortilla - just a bit.

2. Have **cb** place tortillas in the oven for 5 minutes or until they start to crisp. Remove and place on paper plates.

3. Place a small bowl of sauce and a small bowl of mozzarella cheese on the table for each person making their own pizza. First, spread the sauce on with a spoon and then sprinkle with cheese.

4. Have **cb** place pizzas back in oven for 6-8 minutes or until done to your liking. Remove, cool and cut into quarters.

## Did You Know?

Approximately 3 BILLION pizzas are sold in the United States each year.

# Make Your Own Pizza

# Spaghetti Salad

What's in your garden or local farm stand? Use it to create a spaghetti salad in a snap!

## INGREDIENTS

1 pound box spaghetti

Veggies of your choice, cut into cubes (such as tomatoes, carrots, cucumbers, peppers or broccoli)

Black olives, halved (optional)

1 bottle of Italian salad dressing

1. Have **cb** help you cook spaghetti according to package directions. Run cold water over spaghetti to help it cool faster, drain.

2. Place spaghetti into serving bowl and toss with some Italian salad dressing.

3. Wash chosen vegetables. Have **cb** help you cut vegetables into cubes.

4. Combine vegetables and spaghetti, toss with salad dressing and serve.

*Variation:* Your **cb** *can help you to partially sauté thinly sliced or cubed veggies such as zucchini, yellow squash or red onions prior to adding them to salad.*

*Tip: Can be refrigerated for 2 days in a sealed container.*

INSERT PHOTO

Dinner

INSERT PHOTO

Fill tomatoes with your favorite salad: chicken, tuna, macaroni, potato or corn. It's an easy way to make an everyday dish extra special.

## INGREDIENTS

**For Chicken Salad:**

2 cups diced cooked chicken (baked, grilled or boiled)

½ cup diced celery

½ cup dried cranberries

¼ cup sliced almonds (optional)

4 strips crispy bacon, crumbled (optional)

Salt and pepper to taste

Mayonnaise to taste

4 medium tomatoes

1. Combine all ingredients except tomatoes in a medium bowl and toss well. Chill.

**For Tomato Bowls:**

1. Wash and dry tomatoes. Have **cb** help you slice the tops off each tomato. Using the small end of a melon baller or spoon, scrape out most of the inside of each tomato. Be careful not to break through the sides or bottom.

2. Turn the tomato bowls upside down and place onto paper towels. Allow them to drain for 30 minutes.

3. Once drained, turn them over, fill with the chicken salad and serve.

### Did You Know?

There are more chickens on Earth than people.

# Peek-A-Boo Salad

# What's YOUR Favorite Noodle Soup?

Do you have any idea how many different noodles there are? The next time you are at the food store, see how many you can count!

## INGREDIENTS

2 quarts chicken broth

3 cups vegetable broth

1 teaspoon of chicken bouillon

½ cup diced carrots

½ cup diced celery (optional)

1 to 1 ½ cups noodles of your choice (we like ABC or Ditalini – what do you like?)

1. In a large pot, combine chicken broth, vegetable broth, bouillon and vegetables.

2. Place pot on the stove and have **cb** cook on medium-high heat until it boils.

3. Have **cb** help you add the noodles and stir. Boil for an additional 10-15 minutes and have **cb** stir a few times along the way.

4. Have **cb** remove from heat. Let soup sit for 10 minutes, then serve.

*Variations: Add in some cooked chicken, frozen peas or cooked **Mini Meatballs** (p.51) if you like. Just toss in when you turn off the burner and let heat through for 10 minutes*

INSERT PHOTO

Dinner

59

Mashed Potato Pie, 62

Salad Cups, 63

Veggie Bake, 65

Carrot Casserole, 66

# On The Side

Oven Taters, 64

Spinach Balls, 67

INSERT PHOTO

OOH baby, mashed potatoes + pizza dough = perfection!

## INGREDIENTS

Pizza dough

6 strips bacon

3 large potatoes (5 if using red bliss), peeled

2 cups shredded Cheddar cheese

½ cup milk (more or less to taste)

4 tablespoons melted butter

½ teaspoon salt

Pepper to taste

Optional accompaniments;
Sour cream
Green onions (just the greens), chopped

Preheat oven to 350º.

1. Have **cb** boil potatoes for about 20 minutes or until tender and ready to mash. Drain.

2. Have **cb** help you cook the bacon until crispy. Let cool, crumble and set aside.

3. In a lightly greased round baking dish, cake or spring form pan (6-8 inches in diameter; no more than 2 inches deep), spread the pizza dough evenly going up the sides at least half way.

4. Mash potatoes with a potato masher then whip with a hand held mixer adding milk, butter, salt and pepper. Add ½ cup of the cheese.

5. Spread mashed potatoes over the dough; sprinkle with the remaining cheese and the bacon.

6. Have **cb** bake pie for about 20 minutes. Remove from the oven and let rest for a few minutes, then slice and serve. Top with suggested accompaniments.

*Tip: For best results, buy pre-packaged pizza dough.*

# Mashed Potato Pie

# Salad Cups

Usually you need to use a fork to eat your salad – not this time, these go down in 1 or 2 bites!

## INGREDIENTS

10 slices thin white or wheat bread with crusts removed

3 tablespoons melted butter

**Did You Know?**

Thomas Jefferson, the 3rd US President, had 19 varieties of lettuce growing in his garden at his home, Monticello.

Preheat oven to 400º.

1. Have **cb** help you roll out bread slices with a rolling pin, a few rolls in each direction.

2. Cut out 2-3 rounds from each slice of bread using a 3 inch fluted pastry cutter, biscuit cutter or cookie cutter – whatever you have available. (In a pinch, you can use a small glass with a 3-inch opening.)

3. Using a cupcake pan, press a round of bread into each opening, pressing down to form a cup shape. Brush each round with melted butter.

4. Have **cb** bake for 10 minutes or until golden brown. Cool.

5. Fill cups with Caesar salad or your favorite salad tossed in dressing. If using Caesar salad, garnish with a thin slice or sprinkle of Parmesan cheese. For best results, chop up the salad into small pieces.

*Variation: You can chop up tomatoes, cucumbers and carrots, toss in a bit of dressing and fill cups. Any combination of salad ingredients you like will work as long as you cut it small.*

*Tip: If using a mini cupcake pan, use a 2-inch cutter.*

On The Side

INSERT PHOTO

INSERT PHOTO

A potato, a bit of olive oil and some Kosher salt can go a long way!

## INGREDIENTS

2 large baking potatoes

1-2 tablespoons of light olive oil

1 tablespoon Kosher salt, more or less to taste

Preheat oven to 400º.

1. Clean potatoes.

2. Have **cb** slice each potato into 6-8 wedges.

3. Place oil and potatoes in a sealed plastic bag. Gently shake the bag so that the potatoes are completely covered in oil. Remove potatoes from the bag and place on a lightly oiled baking sheet.

4. Sprinkle potato wedges liberally with Kosher salt and have **cb** cook for 10 minutes. Have **cb** flip them and cook for an additional 10 minutes or until they begin to brown and crisp. Sprinkle with another dash of Kosher salt and serve.

*Variation: If you like things spicy...shake a few dashes of hot sauce on these when ready to eat.*

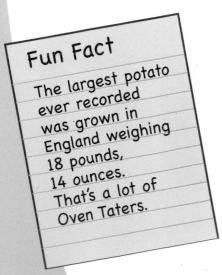

### Fun Fact

The largest potato ever recorded was grown in England weighing 18 pounds, 14 ounces. That's a lot of Oven Taters.

# Oven Taters

# Veggie Bake

I don't know about you, but sometimes we like to disguise our veggies, and this does the trick.

## INGREDIENTS

2 (1 pound) bags frozen vegetable medley, thawed (broccoli, cauliflower, carrots)

1 ½ cups shredded Cheddar cheese

1 cup sour cream

8 ounces softened cream cheese

1 packet vegetable soup/dip mix

Preheat oven to 350º.

1. Drain vegetables.

2. Combine cheese, cream cheese, sour cream and vegetable soup mix in a large bowl and mix well. Add in vegetables and toss until coated.

3. Pour into casserole dish and have **cb** cook for 30 minutes.

*Tip: When ready to serve you can top off with crushed crackers for a different taste.*

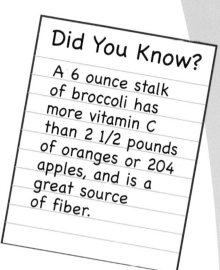

Did You Know?

A 6 ounce stalk of broccoli has more vitamin C than 2 1/2 pounds of oranges or 204 apples, and is a great source of fiber.

INSERT PHOTO

On The Side

INSERT PHOTO

## On The Side

Grow your own carrots and then make this colorful side dish.

### INGREDIENTS

2 pounds carrots, peeled and cut into 1 inch chunks (or use baby carrots in a bag)

2 cups shredded Cheddar cheese

¼ teaspoon pepper

2 eggs, slightly beaten

2 tablespoons of sugar

1 stick of butter

Preheat oven to 350º.

1. Have **cb** help you cook carrots in a pot of water until very soft and easily pierced with a fork, approximately 25 minutes.

2. Have **cb** drain carrots, mash well with a potato masher or place in your blender and puree.

3. Scrape into a bowl and stir in remaining ingredients.

4. Have **cb** bake uncovered for 45 minutes.

### Did You Know?

The carrot gets its characteristic bright orange color from Beta-Carotene.

# Carrot Casserole

# Spinach Balls

Great for snacking or as a side dish. Just pop them in your mouth and enjoy. Watch out for grown ups, they have been known to gobble these up!

## INGREDIENTS

¼ cup butter, melted

1 box frozen chopped spinach, thawed and drained

1 cup seasoned bread crumbs

1 tablespoon dried onion or onion powder

4 ounces Muenster cheese, shredded

Pinch of salt and pepper

¼ teaspoon garlic salt (optional)

3 eggs, beaten

1. Mix together all ingredients and refrigerate until mixture "sets up" (approximately 30-60 minutes).

2. When ready to cook, have **cb** help you form mixture into 1-inch balls, place on baking sheet and bake at 350º for 9 to 11 minutes.

*You can also freeze these uncooked. Just place on a cookie sheet and freeze for about 1 hour, after that place in plastic freezer bags or container. When ready to use, thaw for about 20 minutes then cook as directed.*

## Did You Know?

China is the world's largest spinach producer, responsible for 85% of the world's production.

INSERT PHOTO

On The Side

Ice Cream Pie, 70

Perfect Parfait, 71

Yum Balls, 73

Favorite Yogurt Pie, 74

Triple Me Chocolate, 76

Fruit Jewels, 77

Pirate Cannonballs, 72

# Dessert Please

Orange Delight, 75

No Bake Cheesecake, 78

Chocolate Puddle, 79

INSERT PHOTO

This is a HUGE hit with kids! You get to decorate your own mini pie or work together to create a large one. Don't forget to make one for the grown ups!

## INGREDIENTS

Pre-made crust of your choice (cookie crumb, graham cracker)– look for the mini pre-made crusts so each kid can have his or her own

1 quart of softened ice cream

Choice of 2 or 3 decorative toppings like mini chocolate chips, sprinkles, mini candies, cookie crumbs, etc.

1. Fill pie crust(s) with softened ice cream, spreading evenly.

2. Freeze filled piecrusts for at least 1 hour.

3. When ready to serve, take out of the freezer and let sit for 5 minutes. Fill small bowls with toppings and let each child take a turn selecting their toppings to create their own pie.

**Did You Know?**
It takes 12 pounds of milk to make 1 gallon of ice cream.

# Ice Cream Pie

# Perfect Parfait

This is a perfect ending to a summer barbeque, light and refreshing. A great no cook, quick prep dessert.

## INGREDIENTS

8 ounces
cream cheese, softened
(should be very soft)

16 ounces sour cream

1 tablespoon almond
extract (optional)

1 tablespoon vanilla

1 box instant
vanilla pudding

½ cup sugar

1 can cherry pie filling

1. In a large bowl, add in all ingredients except cherries. Using a hand or stationary mixer, mix on medium speed for 4-5 minutes until rich and thick.

2. To serve, use a medium to large clear glass bowl or use individual sized glasses or glass bowls. Place half of the cheese mixture in serving bowl, top with some of the cherries, then add the rest of the cheese mixture and top off with more cherries. Cover and chill for 1 hour or more prior to serving.

**Fun Facts**

Parfait (par-FAY) is a French word meaning "perfect."

INSERT PHOTO

INSERT PHOTO

Ahoy Mateys!  These here cannonballs are a secret pirate treasure. What did you think they did with all those coconuts anyway? Careful! You never know when a pirate may show up for a taste!

INGREDIENTS

½ cup powdered sugar

1 cup peanut butter

1 cup crispy rice cereal

¼ cup finely shredded coconut

1. In a large bowl, mix peanut butter, powdered sugar and cereal.

2. Using your hands, roll mixture into small 1-inch balls. Place on a wax or parchment paper lined baking sheet.

3. Place coconut in a small bowl and roll balls one at a time in the coconut.  Place balls back on baking sheet and refrigerate for at least 1 hour before serving.

*Variations: You can roll Cannonballs in crushed graham crackers, powdered sugar, or sprinkles.*

### Did You Know?

Every pirate captain had his or her own flag using the colors black, red and white. What would your pirate flag look like?

# Pirate Cannonballs

# Yum Balls

These are quick to make and better to eat. They make a nice gift or treat.

## INGREDIENTS

1 package chocolate cream sandwich cookies

8 ounces cream cheese, softened

14 ounce package of chocolate melting disks (used for candy making: found at craft stores and some supermarkets)

1. Have **cb** help you crush cookies until they are crumbs in a food processor or place in plastic bag and crush with a kid's hammer or mallet.

2. Add softened cream cheese. If using a food processor, have **cb** help you pulse to blend until dough-like ball forms. Otherwise, stir with a large spoon and mix until dough-like ball forms.

3. Roll into small 1-inch balls. Place balls on parchment lined baking sheet and refrigerate for 30 minutes.

4. Roll in chocolate or pastel colored sprinkles, place on parchment lined baking sheet and refrigerate until serving.

INSERT PHOTO

Dessert Please

INSERT PHOTO

Try key lime yogurt with a chocolate crust – one of our favorites!

## INGREDIENTS

Purchased pie shell (graham or chocolate crust)

Two 6 ounce pre-mixed containers of yogurt (strawberry, key lime, blueberry, or lemon)

⅔ of a container of whipped topping, thawed

1. In a medium bowl, mix yogurt and whipped topping. Whisk together until combined.

2. Pour mixture into prepared pie shell. Cover and freeze for 3-4 hours or overnight.

3. Serve frozen or partially thawed.

*Variations: You can leave the top of the pie plain or decorate it with sprinkles, fruit, crushed cookies or whipped cream. Serve frozen or partially thawed for two different tastes.*

# Favorite Yogurt Pie

# Orange Delight

Makes a nice dessert or snack. For something different, serve in scooped out orange halves.

## INGREDIENTS

3 cups water

3 ounce box orange gelatin

3 ounce box cook and serve vanilla pudding

3 ounce box cook and serve tapioca pudding

8 ounce container whipped topping, thawed

1 small can mandarin oranges

1. Pour water into a pot and have **cb** help bring it to a boil.

2. Have **cb** help you add pudding, tapioca and gelatin. Cook over medium heat until thickened. Remove and cool to room temperature.

3. Stir in whipped topping and mandarin oranges. Chill for at least 3 hours and serve.

### Did You Know?

In 1873, three Navel orange trees were brought from Brazil and planted in California. This began the California orange industry.

INSERT PHOTO

INSERT PHOTO

Each part is yummy on its own – but when you combine them all - WOW!

### INGREDIENTS

Brownies

Chocolate pudding, prepared according to package directions

4 of your favorite chocolate candy bars

1 (12 ounce) carton thawed whipped topping

1 ¾ cups milk

1. Cut or break up the brownies into pieces. Set aside.

2. Place candy bars into plastic bag. Using a meat tenderizer, pound to break into little pieces reserving some for the topping.

3. In a large bowl, layer ½ brownies, ½ pudding, ½ candy and ½ whipped topping. Repeat layers. Sprinkle reserved candy on top. Refrigerate until ready to serve.

### Did You Know?

The cacao bean, from which chocolate comes, was so valuable that the Maya, Aztec and Toltec people used it as money.

# Triple Me Chocolate

# Fruit Jewels

Little tarts that sparkle and taste great too! We can't decide our favorite part – the cookie, the fruit or the glaze.

## INGREDIENTS

1 stick butter (¼ pound), room temperature

½ cup sugar

1 egg yolk

1 tablespoon orange juice

1 teaspoon vanilla extract

1 ¾ cups flour

3 cups fruit such as: sliced bananas, grapes halved, strawberries, whole or sliced, blueberries, mandarin oranges (drained) or try your favorite fruit.

Preheat oven to 350º.

1. In a medium bowl, have **cb** help you beat butter until fluffy. Gradually mix in sugar, beating until light and fluffy. Add in egg yolk, orange juice and vanilla. Mix in flour until a dough like ball forms.

2. Have **cb** help you press bits of dough into 2 or 3 inch tartlett molds or a cupcake pan.

3. Bake for 15-20 minutes or until lightly browned. Cool for 15 minutes. Have **cb** help you remove tarts from mold by using the tip of a butter knife inserted between edge of crust and mold. Pop into your hand. Place on cooling rack to cool completely.

**For Glaze:**
½ cup sugar
3 ½ teaspoons of cornstarch
1 cup of orange juice

1. Mix sugar, cornstarch and orange juice in a small pot and stir until smooth. Have **cb** help you heat to a boil, stirring constantly. Keep at a boil for about 2 minutes, until thickened. Cover and cool.

2. Fill tart shells with your chosen fruit(s). Spoon cooled glaze over tops of each. For best results, eat these the day you make them.

INSERT PHOTO

Dessert Please

INSERT PHOTO

This is a fantastic first cheesecake. After you master making this one, move on to one you bake!

## INGREDIENTS

8 ounces of cream cheese, softened

2 teaspoons of vanilla

8 ounces of whipped topping, thawed

1 cup of sour cream

⅓ cup of sugar

Pre-made crust of your choice

1. In a large bowl with mixer on medium speed, beat cream cheese and sugar until well mixed. Add in sour cream, vanilla and whipped topping. Mix well.

2. Pour into crust and refrigerate overnight.

*Variations: You can serve this plain, topped with whipped cream, pie filling, fresh fruit or chocolate shavings.*

### Did You Know?

Cheesecake is believed to have originated in ancient Greece. It was served to the athletes during the first Olympic Games held in 776 B.C.

# No Bake Cheesecake

# Chocolate Puddle

If you think it's great jumping in puddles, try dunking in puddles.

## INGREDIENTS

1 cup of chocolate chips

⅔ cup corn syrup

½ cup heavy cream

*Any or all of the following dunkers:*

Pound cake cut into 1-inch squares

Pineapple chunks

Apple wedges

Banana chunks

Strawberry halves

Grapes

Marshmallows

Animal crackers

Mini pretzel sticks

1. Arrange any or all of the dunkers on a big platter leaving room in the center for 1 or 2 small bowls for chocolate.

2. In a medium saucepan, have **cb** help you heat the cream and corn syrup. Stir constantly until boiling.

3. Have **cb** remove from heat. Have **cb** help you carefully add chocolate chips. Stir until melted. Serve right away.

*Tip: Everyone loves this. Hands are reaching and dipping quickly. Depending on how many you are serving, you may want to set up individual "puddles".*

INSERT PHOTO

Insert family photo here.

# My Family Recipes

## Add your own family recipes.

For best results when writing your family recipes in this section, please use a ballpoint pen. If using a marker, please allow the page to dry for 15 seconds before touching the ink or turning the page.

# My Family Recipes

RECIPE NAME

INGREDIENTS

DIRECTIONS

NOTES

RECIPE NAME

INGREDIENTS

DIRECTIONS

NOTES

# My Family Recipes

RECIPE NAME

INGREDIENTS

DIRECTIONS

NOTES

RECIPE NAME

INGREDIENTS

DIRECTIONS

NOTES

My Family Recipes

# Index

# Index

## Wax Paper vs. Parchment Paper

Waxed paper and parchment paper may appear to be the same, however they have different uses. Wax paper is coated with wax to prevent sticking. Use wax paper to cover your counter when rolling out cookie dough, when lining a box or container of candy or cookies, to catch food when grating or as a no mess spoon rest.

Parchment paper is paper that is coated with silicone, making it moisture and grease resistant. Unlike waxed paper, it can withstand exposure to temperatures up to 420°F in the oven. Parchment paper may brown when exposed to oven heat, but won't burn. It should not be used in ovens heated above 420°F or under the broiler. Parchment paper is used to line baking sheets when making cookies, pastries or anything with cheese. It can also be used to create piping bags for cake decorating. Parchment paper makes cleanup a snap. When finished, just crumble and toss into the trash.

On a rare "girls night out" an idea was shared and an adventure began. Eleven months later, **Picture Me Cooking™** was born! Each of us is someone's daughter, mother, spouse and friend. Looking for a way to show another piece of who we are, we poured ourselves into creating this book as well as what will follow. It has been an interesting journey, we have learned so much along the way, made new friends and added a couple of pounds (you know how it goes . . . who do you think tasted these recipes over and over). We have proven to ourselves that we can juggle our families, careers, friendships and lives and still find time to create something we believe in.

So grab the nearest kid and camera, head for your kitchen and cook up some *fun!*

| Rebecca Dubas Rice | Amanda R. Coopersmith | Maureen Miley Petrie | Colleen Kennedy |

Thanks to Deb and Krista for putting up with us…the idea became tangible
and it would not have happened without you both.

Steph, thanks for always being there with advice.

To our spouses, children, parents and siblings: thank you all for your opinions
and for putting up with our chatter about the project.

To our waistlines: Sorry for all the taste testing along the way.

Becky and Tate: Thanks for the many times we overtook your kitchen.

To Bonnie and Eric who opened the door to help us realize our dream.

To Steve who believed in us from the beginning and never stopped! Thank you is not enough.
Who knew what could be accomplshed at grocery store cafe's!

To Scott who knows a good thing when he sees it! Thank you.